YORK NOTES
KEY STAGE 3

Henry V

William Shakespeare
Note by David Langston

 Longman

York Press

York Press
322 Old Brompton Road, London SW5 9JH

Pearson Education Limited
Edinburgh Gate, Harlow, Essex CM20 2JE, United Kingdom
Associated companies, branches and representatives throughout
the world

First published 2000
ISBN 0-582-43147-6

Illustrated by Judy Stevens
Designed by Vicki Pacey
Phototypeset by Gem Graphics, Trenance, Mawgan Porth, Cornwall
Produced by Pearson Education China Limited, Hong Kong

Contents

Preface

York Notes Key Stage 3 guides are designed to give you the help you need to tackle the plays of Shakespeare, a requirement for the National Tests.

The English tests (sometimes called SATs) are taken in the final term of Year 9. Pupils must sit two papers: Paper 1 on Reading and Writing and Paper 2 on Key Scenes taken from a Shakespeare play chosen by your teacher. The papers are marked by external examiners and the results are published at the end of July, in the form of a Level for English.

KEY SCENE

This symbol shows the Key Scenes which form the core of the play

Each of these Notes will provide a biography of Shakespeare and close examination of one of the set plays, and include a summary of each scene in the play as well as detailed summaries of the Key Scenes on which the National Test focuses. To check your progress, tests are included on each Act. Commentary is also provided on themes, characters and language.

York Notes Key Stage 3 are written by English teachers and examiners with an expert knowledge of the subject. They show you how to succeed in your Key Stage 3 tests, taking you through the play and offering practical guidance.

York Notes Key Stage 3 guides are ideal for
* Understanding Shakespeare
* Preparing for exams
* Improving your Level

The author of this Note is David Langston. He is a part-time lecturer in Adult Education, a former head of English and an examiner at GCSE and Key Stage 3 for a major examination board. He has written and contributed to GCSE textbooks.

The text used in this Note is the Arden Shakespeare, edited by T.W. Craik (Routledge, 1995).

Introduction

How to study a Shakespeare play

The National Curriculum in English makes it compulsory for Key Stage 3 students to study for an examination on a Shakespeare play. This book aims to guide you through this task by explaining carefully the development of the story of your chosen play, and by setting out the important features which you will need to include in your examination response.

Shakespeare wrote his plays for performance on a stage. The best way in to this play is of course to go to a theatre and see it live. If you are unable to do this, then hire it on a video or listen to it on audiotape or CD.

One of the chief reasons for the greatness of these plays is that they are entertaining. They are studied in class because their true quality may not be revealed in a single visit to the theatre.

Use the points given below as a check-list to help you to a fuller understanding of what the play is about:

* Follow the story-line – who are the winners and losers? Does the story end in the way you would have chosen? Or would you change its ending? Why?
* Look at the characters – which ones do you like and which ones do you dislike? Are you happy with what happens to them at the end of the play?
* Look at the staging of the play – is the set what you would have expected? If not, why not? Do you think that you might have been mistaken in your view of what the set should have been? Why?
* Look at the costumes – are they what you would have expected? Again, if not, why not? Do the characters' costumes tell you anything about the characters themselves?

∗   Think of the special effects, like lighting and sound –
    what did they add to your enjoyment of the production?

    Remember each generation interprets Shakespeare in a
    way that makes sense to its audiences. If you see
    Shakespeare's plays as museum pieces, you are unlikely
    to be very entertained by them.

    Think about this: the best students are those who
    identify with the plays they watch. What do you think
    this play can tell you about life in the new millennium?

    Find answers to that question and you will truly
    have made a success of your first experience with
    Shakespeare study.

Shakespeare's life

Family life

William Shakespeare was born at Stratford-upon-Avon in 1564. There is a record of his christening on 26 April, so we can assume he was born shortly before that date. His father, John Shakespeare, was a glove-maker and trader who later became high bailiff of Stratford; his mother, Mary Arden, was the daughter of a landowner.

In 1582 Shakespeare married Anne Hathaway, a woman eight years older than himself. Their first child, Susanna, was christened in May 1583, and in 1585 twins Hamnet and Judith were born.

Shakespeare lived during the reign of Queen Elizabeth I, a period known as the Elizabethan Age.

Writing

Sometime after 1585 Shakespeare left Stratford and went to London where he became an actor and a dramatist. He worked first with a group of actors called Lord Pembroke's Men and later with a company called the Lord Chamberlain's Men (later the King's Men). His earliest plays were performed around 1590 to 1594. He was successful in the theatre from the start.

In 1599 Shakespeare wrote the history play *Henry V*.

The last years

Although Shakespeare lived and worked for most of his life in London, he obviously did not forget Stratford, and in about 1610 he returned to live there permanently.

Shakespeare wrote a will in January 1616, leaving money to people he knew in Stratford and to some of his actor-friends. He died on 23 April 1616.

Background to the play

After the defeat of the Spanish Armada in 1588 there was an increase in patriotic feeling in the country

Queen Elizabeth I reigned from 1558 to 1603. During the later years of her rule, when Shakespeare was writing his history plays, there were constant fears of plots and rebellions.

The issues of stable monarchy, rank and order in society, unity, loyalty, rebellion and treason are significant themes in a number of Shakespeare's plays of this period. In Henry V we see the King check the legitimacy of his rights to France, act firmly on those rights, deal with treachery, unite and inspire his people and maintain a firm and just control.

When Henry V was first performed, the Earl of Tyrone had recently led a rebellion against the English forces in Ireland. Queen Elizabeth appointed the popular Earl of Essex as governor of Ireland and he set off to suppress the rebels. There is a reference to his expected victorious return at the beginning of Act V, lines 29–32. Henry goes to France to claim his rights and Essex goes to Ireland to do the same on behalf of the Queen.

Elizabethan society

In the sixteenth century, the population of London grew from 50,000 to 200,000, despite a serious outbreak of plague. It was a centre of trade and commerce and also a focus for those who wished to find favour at court. At the other end of the social scale it was home to a large criminal underclass of thieves, professional beggars, swindlers, prostitutes, pimps and brothel-keepers.

In *Henry IV, Part 1* and *Part 2*, Shakespeare shows us this underworld through his amusing portraits of the low-life characters. Some of these characters survive in Henry V and see the military campaign as an opportunity to extend their thieving into new areas.

Summaries

Act I

Chorus

Introduction
to the play

The play opens with a Prologue spoken by the Chorus. He calls for inspiration to help show the great events and heroic characters involved in the story that is to be presented. He asks the audience to make allowances for the limitations of the small theatre and encourages them to use their imaginations to conjure up the large number of men and horses involved in the battles.

Comment

The Chorus was used in classical Greek drama to comment on the action and usually consisted of a group of actors. In this play, the Chorus is spoken by a single actor.

Shakespeare wishes to make clear to his audience that they are about to see a story about a great man.

Scene 1

Two
churchmen
discuss the
King

The Archbishop of Canterbury and the Bishop of Ely are discussing the re-introduction of a government bill which will strip the Church of a great deal of its wealth. The Archbishop is pleased that the King seems to be in sympathy with them and has been offered a substantial gift of money.

We hear that the King's character has reformed since he has come to the throne and that he is widely admired and respected.

The Archbishop reveals the King's claims to the crown of France and the presence of French Ambassadors at the court.

Comment

We see that the churchmen have a strong motive for encouraging the King's claims in France. If they help pay for the war, it will turn attention away from the bill that threatens to take away their wealth.

The description of the changes in King Henry's character remind the audience of his wild and reckless behaviour as Prince Hal in the previous two plays in the series, *Henry IV, Part 1* and *Part 2*. The audience will be interested to see this reformed King living up to the promises he made in *Henry IV, Part 1* (Act I, Scene 2).

The main plot of the King's claim to the crown of France is introduced and we know there will be trouble between Henry and the French Ambassadors.

| Scene 2 | King Henry sends for the Archbishop of Canterbury and asks him for his opinion on his claims in France. He warns the Archbishop that a great deal of blood may be shed as a consequence of his advice. |

KEY SCENE

The Salic law

The Archbishop gives a detailed history of the kingdoms of France and Germany. He mentions the Salic law, which prevents females from claiming the throne. This law has been used by the French to deny Henry's claim, but it is valid only in Germany and does not apply in France.

Henry asks the Archbishop to confirm his right to make the claim. He does and reminds him of his ancestors' victories against the French and promises a generous donation from the Church.

Some of the nobles present add their encouragement. The King then considers the possibility that the Scots may take advantage of his absence and invade England. The Archbishop, using as a **metaphor** (see Literary Terms) the different functions of bees in a bee-hive, suggests that the King should divide his forces into four and take one quarter with him to France. Henry says he is determined to rule France or to die in the attempt.

Henry's claim to the French crown

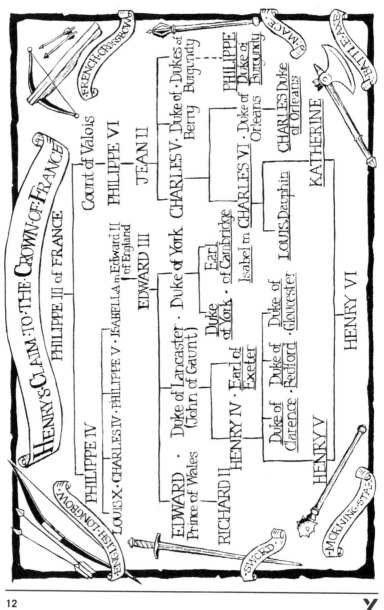

HENRY'S CLAIM TO THE CROWN OF FRANCE

PHILIPPE III of FRANCE

Count of Valois — PHILIPPE VI — JEAN II — CHARLES V · Duke of · Dukes of — PHILIPPE · Duke of Burgundy
                                                                        Berry Burgundy   Duke of Burgundy

PHILIPPE IV

LOUIS X · CHARLES IV · PHILIPPE V · ISABELLA m Edward II of England

EDWARD III

Duke of York   CHARLES VI · Duke of Orleans   CHARLES Duke of Orleans

KATHERINE

EDWARD Prince of Wales   Duke of Lancaster (John of Gaunt)   Earl of Cambridge   Isabel m CHARLES VI   LOUIS, Dauphin

Duke of York

RICHARD II   HENRY IV · Earl of Exeter   Duke of Bedford · Duke of Gloucester   HENRY VI

Duke of Clarence · Duke of Bedford · Duke of Gloucester

HENRY V

FRENCH·CROSSBOW

·MACE·

BATTLE·AXE·

ENGLISH·LONGBOW·

·SWORD·

·MORNING·STAR·

The French
Ambassadors
enter

The French Ambassadors are shown in. They are from the Dauphin, son of the French King. Henry assures them that they may speak plainly. The Dauphin's message is an insulting rejection of Henry's claims to French dukedoms and refers to his reputation as a trivial pleasure-seeker. This message is accompanied by a mocking gift of tennis balls, suggesting that he should go and play games.

King Henry takes up the theme of tennis in his reply and warns that a more deadly game will follow. He says that his life so far has merely been preparation for taking his place on the throne of France. The Dauphin's mockery will only bring misery and hardship on the French people as Henry intends to proceed in a just cause.

When the Ambassadors are dismissed Henry tells his followers to prepare for the expedition.

Comment

King Henry wants religious and legal support for his claim. He makes the Archbishop share the responsibility for the proposed war.

The Archbishop gives his legal opinion but also encourages Henry with references to his heroic ancestors. Both the Archbishop and the Bishop of Ely use bloodthirsty images.

Henry shows that he is a cautious and responsible ruler when he considers the danger of a Scottish invasion.

Henry's reply to the Dauphin's message shows dignity, self-control and wit. There is also a cold, menacing determination in his speech.

The nobles and Church are united behind an intelligent and formidable young monarch.

Test (Act I)

a Fill in the blanks

The play is opened by the .... who asks the .... to forgive the limitations of the smalll .... and to use their imaginations to supply the large numbers of men and .... engaged in the ....

Two church leaders are talking. They say that the character of .... has greatly improved since he became ....

He led a wild and reckless life before he came to the ....

Henry now wishes to claim the throne of ....

After listening to advice from the church leaders and .... , King Henry decides to .... France. The French .... are brought in and they deliver an insulting gift of .... from the .... Henry sends a stern reply and tells his nobles to prepare for ....

b Give modern words for these words used by Shakespeare

1 casques (Prologue.13)
2 puissance (Prologue.25)
3 lazars (I.1.15)
4 riots (I.1.56)
5 nicely (I.2.15)
6 marches (I.2.140)
7 giddy (I.2.145)
8 congreeing (I.2.182)
9 wrangler (I.2.265)
10 proportions (I.2.305)

C Quiz

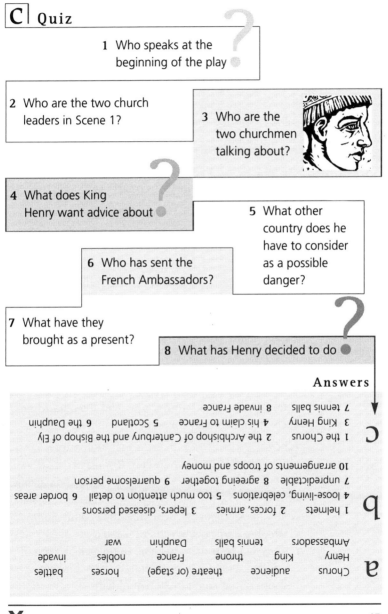

1 Who speaks at the beginning of the play

2 Who are the two church leaders in Scene 1?

3 Who are the two churchmen talking about?

4 What does King Henry want advice about

5 What other country does he have to consider as a possible danger?

6 Who has sent the French Ambassadors?

7 What have they brought as a present?

8 What has Henry decided to do

Answers

C
1 the Chorus   **2** the Archbishop of Canterbury and the Bishop of Ely
3 King Henry   **4** his claim to France   **5** Scotland   **6** the Dauphin
7 tennis balls   **8** invade France

b
1 helmets   **2** forces, armies   **3** lepers, diseased persons
4 loose-living, celebrations   **5** too much attention to detail   **6** border areas
7 unpredictable   **8** agreeing together   **9** quarrelsome person
10 arrangements of troops and money

a
Chorus	audience	theatre (or stage)	horses	battles
Henry	King	throne	France	nobles	invade
Ambassadors	tennis balls	Dauphin	war

Y   **15**

Act II

Chorus

News of
traitors

The Chorus tells us about the excitement and anticipation in England as the King and his followers prepare for war. We learn that the French have bribed three English traitors to murder Henry before he sets sail. When we next see the King he will be in Southampton.

Comment

The business-like preparations of the English contrast with the vanity and show of the French nobles later in the play.

The audience will be curious about the outcome of the murder plot.

Scene 1

A quarrel
between
low-life
characters

In a street, Bardolph and Nym, two of the old drinking companions of King Henry's youth, meet and discuss Nym's quarrel with Pistol, another low-life character. Pistol is married to Nell Quickly, hostess of a tavern, who had previously been engaged to Nym. These three rogues are about to set off on the expedition to France.

When Pistol enters with his wife, he and Nym exchange extravagant and ludicrous insults and threaten to fight each other. Bardolph comes between them.

A boy servant enters with news that his master is very ill and begs them to come to him. (His master is Sir John Falstaff, another of the King's old drinking companions, now cast off by the reformed and responsible monarch.) Nell Quickly leaves with the Boy and Bardolph establishes a truce between Pistol and Nym. The Hostess returns and begs them to come to the sick Sir John. It is suggested that he is suffering from a broken heart because of the King's treatment of him.

Comment

These low-life characters bring humour to the play and their scenes provide light relief from the serious events of the main plot.

The audience is reminded of the King's wild youth by the presence of these old companions who show the great changes in his behaviour.

Pistol speaks in a pompous, comical kind of verse. It is a windy parody of epic style, full of alliteration (see Literary Terms) and suits his boastful, empty bravado.

Scene 2

KEY SCENE

Henry exposes the traitors

At Southampton, some of the English lords are discussing the traitors in their midst when the King enters with the three conspirators. He asks their opinion of the prospects for his invasion of France. They answer with encouraging words and he says he will not forget to reward people according to what they deserve.

Henry orders the release of a drunk who was arrested for shouting insults about him in the streets, but the traitors protest that he is being too lenient. He then hands the traitors written orders that reveal their treachery. They immediately fall on their knees and ask for his mercy. Henry says that they have just advised him against being too merciful. He denounces them for their treason, particularly Lord Scroop who had been close to him.

The traitors will be executed

The traitors repent and accept their fate. King Henry sentences them to death and they are taken away to be executed. The discovery of the plot is seen by Henry as a sign that God is on his side and he orders the immediate departure of the invasion fleet.

Comment

At the beginning of the scene we share the knowledge with the King and his lords that the plot has been discovered and we are anxious to see how the traitors will be exposed and how they will react.

Henry shows his command of the situation by playing with the traitors.

We see that Henry is firm in his punishment of serious crimes and confident enough to be merciful in the case of the drunk.

Scene 3

KEY SCENE

Pistol, Bardolph, Nym and the Boy are leaving London to join the army. Pistol's wife, the Hostess, is seeing them off and she gives a pathetic and comic account of the death of Falstaff. Pistol warns her to take good care of business. The rogues leave for France, intending to profit from the war.

Comment

Falstaff's death marks the end of an era. He was the leader and the inspiration of this band of thieves and rogues.

This scene provides another short relief from the serious action.

Pistol's image of going to France to suck blood is a suitable one as they intend to steal what they can, like parasites.

Scene 4

The French organise their defences

At the French court, the French King orders his nobles and his son to strengthen the defences against the English invasion. The Dauphin agrees that precautions should be taken but refuses to accept that the English King is a serious threat. He brushes aside a warning from the Constable of France who believes that Henry has changed. His father the King treats the invasion as a grave danger and refers to previous English successes.

The Duke of Exeter arrives as Ambassador for King Henry. He demands that Charles surrender the crown of France and he hands him a family tree which proves the justice of Henry's claim. Refusal will bring about great suffering and death. King Charles says he will give his answer on the following day.

Exeter then tells the Dauphin that King Henry wishes him to know that he will regret his insulting gift.

Test (Act II)

a Fill in the blanks

The Chorus tells us that next time we see King Henry he will be in .... and warns us that there are .... in the English ranks. We see some of the King's old drinking companions quarrel in the street and we learn that ....
is ill.

At Southampton the King exposes the .... and calls on his nobles to follow him to .... and prepare for war.

At the French court, ... is worried. His son, the .... , believes that King Henry is weak and foolish.

The .... of France disagrees. The Duke of .... brings a message from .... demanding the French crown.

b Give modern words for these words used by Shakespeare

1	dalliance (II.Prologue.2)	6	distemper (II.2.54)
2	wink (II.1.7)	7	gulled (II.2.121)
3	wight (II.1.61)	8	meet (II.4.15)
4	espouse (II.1.78)	9	ordinance (II.4.126)
5	railed (II.2.41)	10	greener (II.4.136)

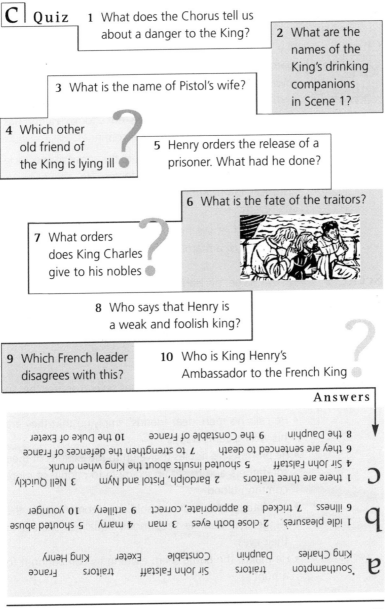

C Quiz

1 What does the Chorus tell us about a danger to the King?

2 What are the names of the King's drinking companions in Scene 1?

3 What is the name of Pistol's wife?

4 Which other old friend of the King is lying ill

5 Henry orders the release of a prisoner. What had he done?

6 What is the fate of the traitors?

7 What orders does King Charles give to his nobles

8 Who says that Henry is a weak and foolish king?

9 Which French leader disagrees with this?

10 Who is King Henry's Ambassador to the French King

Answers

C
1 there are three traitors   2 Bardolph, Pistol and Nym   3 Nell Quickly
4 Sir John Falstaff   5 shouted insults about the King when drunk
6 they are sentenced to death   7 to strengthen the defences of France
8 the Dauphin   9 the Constable of France   10 the Duke of Exeter

b
1 idle pleasures   2 close both eyes   3 man   4 marry   5 shouted abuse
6 illness   7 tricked   8 appropriate, correct   9 artillery   10 younger

a
Southampton   Dauphin   Constable   Exeter   Sir John Falstaff   traitors   France   King Charles   King Henry

Act III

Chorus

The English besiege Harfleur

The Chorus asks the audience to imagine they have watched the English fleet, like a floating city, sailing towards Harfleur. We are told of the siege of that town and of the French King's offer of his daughter in marriage together with some dukedoms. Henry has rejected the offer and the siege continues.

The Chorus is used to help create the sense of spectacle and the movement of great forces. He also gives us historical information, which helps us to understand later events.

This is the first we hear of Princess Katherine and the suggestion of a marriage between her and Henry.

Scene 1

At the siege of Harfleur, King Henry rallies his men for one more attack on the town. He calls on them to summon up their most fierce and aggressive qualities and reminds them of the victories of their forefathers.

Comment

To achieve his purpose Henry uses several approaches in his speech:
- He calls his men 'dear friends', implying that they are his willing companions
- He prompts his nobles to live up to the exploits of their forefathers and to set an example to people of more common blood
- He flatters the ordinary soldiers (yeomen) with the suggestion that he sees 'noble' qualities shining in their eyes
- He makes the battle seem exciting by comparing it to a hunt

Scene 2

KEY SCENE

The low-life characters avoid the fighting

Bardolph leads the low-life characters at the tail-end of the attack, but Nym, Pistol and the Boy are reluctant to go any further. Fluellen, a Welsh captain, arrives and drives the three rogues forward. The Boy is left on stage. He says that he is tired of working for such cowards and thieves and he plans to find better employment.

A comic discussion of warfare

Fluellen returns and meets Gower, an English captain. They discuss the progress of the mines that are being dug to blow up the town walls. Fluellen expresses contempt for captain Macmorris, an Irishman, who is in charge of the work. Macmorris arrives with Captain Jamy, a Scotsman, and a comical discussion follows. Captain Gower is trying to keep the peace between Fluellen and Macmorris when they are interrupted by the sound of a trumpet-call from the town.

Comment

We witness the cowardly behaviour of the rogues and their undignified retreat from Fluellen's anger.

We have some sympathy for the Boy as he says he does not wish to be corrupted by the thieves.

Shakespeare's audience would have found the language of the captains amusing. They are national stereotypes. The fact that they are having a serious dispute about the technical aspects of warfare in their comic dialects adds to the humour.

The presence of English, Irish, Scots and Welsh captains suggests a broad base of British support for Henry, which reflects the political circumstances of Shakespeare's time. The captains take their work seriously and are loyal soldiers.

Scene 3

Harfleur surrenders

At the gate of Harfleur, King Henry addresses the Governor of Harfleur. He tells him that this is his last chance to surrender and describes in vivid terms the destruction and murder that will follow if the English troops are let loose in the town. The Governor has been told that the Dauphin is unable to send him reinforcements and he surrenders to Henry.

The King leaves the Duke of Exeter in charge of the town with instructions to be merciful to the people. His army has been weakened through sickness and he intends to withdraw to Calais for the winter.

Scene 4

Princess Katherine tries to learn English

Speaking in French, Princess Katherine asks her maid to teach her English. The maid, whose command of English is very poor, tells her the names of parts of the body and Katherine tries to memorise them. Some of the English words sound rather indecent to French ears and the Princess is shocked.

Scene 5

KEY SCENE

The Dauphin and the French nobles are eager to attack the English. They are angry and insulted by the presence of Henry's troops and express contempt for the cold and damp little island they have come from. According to

y

The French
are eager to
attack

the Dauphin the French ladies have begun to mock their menfolk for their lack of courage.

The French King orders his nobles to attack the English and to capture Henry but refuses to allow the Dauphin to go with the army. The Constable of France regrets that, because the English army is so small and weak, Henry will probably surrender without a fight.

| Comment

The French despise the English and consider their kings to be illegitimate sons of France.

They describe the country and the climate in insulting terms. The audience will be keen to see them humbled.

The French use oaths in their conversation, unlike Henry who is pious and dignified in his speech.

King Charles's list of the French nobility who are to attack the English is echoed later in the list of the dead and prisoners after Agincourt (Act IV, Scene 8).

Scene 6

KEY
SCENE

Bardolph is
to be
executed for
stealing

At the English camp, Fluellen meets Captain Gower and tells him about some fighting he has been involved in, defending a bridge with the Duke of Exeter. He says that he noted the bravery of one particular man in the action. This turns out to be Pistol, who arrives to ask Fluellen to go to the Duke of Exeter and talk to him on behalf of Bardolph who is about to be hanged for stealing from a church. Fluellen believes in strict discipline and refuses to interfere. Pistol curses him and leaves. Gower says he recognises Pistol as a well-known rogue, the kind of man who will return to England and live off his tales of the war. Fluellen agrees that Pistol had deceived him.

King Henry enters and Fluellen reports the Duke of Exeter's successful action at the bridge. When asked about English casualties Fluellen says that the only loss is a man called Bardolph, about to be hanged for theft. Even though this was one of his old companions Henry expresses his approval and orders that there is to be no theft from or abuse of the French people.

Montjoy, the French herald, arrives with a message from the King of France. King Charles wishes to know how much Henry is prepared to pay in ransom, though he doubts if the English can afford to raise a sum that would compensate for the damage they have done. He also maintains that Henry has betrayed his followers by leading them to their doom in France.

Henry
declares he
will fight

Henry compliments Montjoy and sends a very honest reply to King Charles. He says that his army is weakened through sickness and he wishes to avoid a fight and return to Calais. However, he will fight if anyone stands in his way. After Montjoy leaves, Henry expresses the view that they are in God's hands and orders his men to make camp.

Comment

Fluellen's report of the action at the bridge helps to give the impression of a moving campaign and the feeling that the audience is seeing part of a larger series of events.

The decline of Henry's old companions is almost complete with Bardolph's execution for this most despicable petty theft. The King's ready support for the hanging shows how completely he has turned his back on the low life.

Montjoy is one of the French characters who gains our respect. Henry admires his courage and dignity.

Henry shows some of his kingly qualities in this scene. He is firm in imposing discipline in his army, generous in his praise of good conduct, even in an enemy, honest in

Y

his dealings with King Charles, humble in his trust in God and brave in the face of danger.

Scene 7

KEY SCENE

The French are very confident

At night in the French camp, some of the nobles are boasting about their horses and armour. They are waiting impatiently for morning and expect an easy victory over the English. The Dauphin, who has now joined the campaign, tries to outdo the others in praise of his horse and the conversation turns into an idle exchange of witticisms. One of the nobles, Rambures, suggests a game of dice for the ransoms of the prisoners they expect to capture. After the Dauphin leaves to put on his armour, the Constable expresses doubts about his bravery.

A messenger reports that the English are camped nearby. The Constable expresses pity for King Henry and both he and Orleans feel that it is sheer stupidity that keeps the English from running away. Orleans anticipates a rich haul of prisoners.

Comment

There is no obvious leader among the French forces. The Dauphin, who is the most senior in rank, does not have the wholehearted support or respect of his nobles.

The Constable's remarks about the Dauphin are quite witty but they are destructive and show he has no confidence in the royal prince.

The French pass their time in idle boasting and gossip. This contrasts with King Henry's serious, practical approach.

The French are so overconfident that they talk of the number of English prisoners they will capture.

The French use images of animals when discussing the English soldiers, which suggests they think of them as being less than human.

Test (Act III)

a Fill in the blanks

The English fleet sails towards the French port of
....

Outside the walls, ... rallies his
troops for one last attack on the town. He asks them to
imitate the action of the ....

Bardolph , ... and Nym are hanging back from
the attack. They are driven forward by Captain
....

The French King gives orders that his army are to attack
the English but he refuses to let the .... go
to war.

Pistol asks .... to speak to the Duke of
.... to prevent the execution of ....
who has been caught stealing from a church.

King Henry tells the French herald .... that he
wishes to avoid a battle and take his army to
.... but the English will fight if they have to.

b Give modern words for these words used by Shakespeare

1 hempen (III.Prologue.8)
2 portage (III.1.10)
3 cullions (III.2.21)
4 antics (III.2.31)
5 bootless (III.3.24)

6 spitted (III.3.38)
7 slobbery (III.5.13)
8 mettle (III.5.29)
9 kern (III.7.53)
10 strossers (III.7.54)

C Quiz

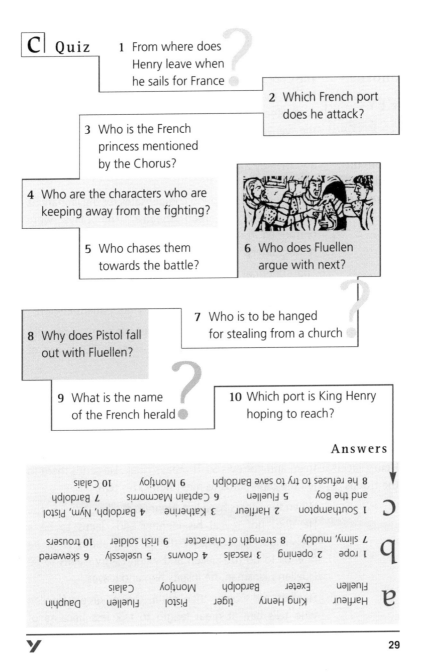

1 From where does Henry leave when he sails for France

2 Which French port does he attack?

3 Who is the French princess mentioned by the Chorus?

4 Who are the characters who are keeping away from the fighting?

5 Who chases them towards the battle?

6 Who does Fluellen argue with next?

7 Who is to be hanged for stealing from a church

8 Why does Pistol fall out with Fluellen?

9 What is the name of the French herald

10 Which port is King Henry hoping to reach?

Answers

C 1 Southampton 2 Harfleur 3 Katherine 4 Bardolph, Nym, Pistol and the Boy 5 Fluellen 6 Captain Macmorris 7 Bardolph 8 he refuses to try to save Bardolph 9 Montjoy 10 Calais

b 1 rope 2 opening 3 rascals 4 clowns 5 uselessly 6 skewered 7 slimy, muddy 8 strength of character 9 Irish soldier 10 trousers

a Harfleur King Henry tiger Pistol Fluellen Dauphin Fluellen Exeter Bardolph Montjoy Calais

Act IV

Chorus

The night
before the
battle

The Chorus describes the sights and sounds of the night before the battle as the two armies are camped near each other. He contrasts the overconfident French with the war-weary English who seem like ghosts. We hear that Henry is visiting his soldiers and that his confident and friendly manner gives them comfort.

Comment

The Chorus's description compensates for the limitations of the Shakespearean theatre. The plays were performed in daylight with few sound effects and little or no scenery.

The unequal nature of the coming contest is emphasised, as is the difference in attitude between the boastful French and the weary but patient English.

Henry's relationship with his troops is seen as friendly, comforting and inspiring. His glance is like a ray of sunshine.

Scene 1

Henry meets
the troops

At night, King Henry is discussing with the Duke of Gloucester the dangerous position they are in, when they meet the Duke of Bedford and Sir Thomas Erpingham, an elderly knight. Henry talks cheerfully to them and borrows Sir Thomas's cloak. He sends them to tell the other lords to meet him in his tent.

When the others have left, Henry is challenged by Pistol. He does not reveal his identity and claims to be a Welshman. This causes Pistol to brag about what he intends to do to Fluellen and when Henry claims to be Fluellen's kinsman, he insults him and leaves.

Fluellen and Gower then enter. Gower greets Fluellen who tells him at great length to talk less because of the nearness of the enemy. They leave without seeing Henry.

Three ordinary soldiers, Court, Bates and Williams, enter. Dawn is breaking and they view it with apprehension. When they see Henry he pretends to be a soldier under Sir Thomas Erpingham's command. They discuss the King and his responsibilities. Bates thinks the King would rather be up to the neck in the River Thames than here in France. Henry disagrees. Bates then says he would prefer that the King was on his own and could be ransomed without loss of life. Henry says that he would be happy to die with the King because his cause is just.

Bates and Williams say that they are there because they are the King's subjects. The King will carry the responsibility if any of his men die in sin. Henry argues that each man is responsible to God for his own sins and the state of his soul and should therefore prepare himself before the battle so that he may die in a state of grace or live on as an example to others.

Williams expresses doubts about the King's intention to refuse personal ransom to save his life and he and Henry quarrel over this. They agree to settle their differences after the battle and exchange gloves, which they will wear in their hats so as to recognise one another. Bates reminds them that they have enough French enemies to deal with.

Henry considers his responsibilities When the soldiers leave, Henry speaks his thoughts about the heavy burdens of kingship. He questions the value of ceremony and the trappings of royalty and compares the uneasy responsibilities of power with the simple, irresponsible life of the slave who can sleep peacefully each night.

Sir Thomas Erpingham arrives to tell Henry that his nobles are looking for him. He says he will meet them at his tent. Alone again, Henry prays to God to give his soldiers courage. He asks God not to punish him on this particular day for the sins of his father. (Henry IV had deposed Richard II who was later murdered.) Henry says he has done his best to compensate for this. He has wept, paid for prayers to be said and has built two chapels dedicated to Richard. He promises to do more. The Duke of Gloucester comes to take him to the meeting.

Comment

We see the friendly relationship between Henry and his nobles and his obvious affection for the elderly Sir Thomas.

Pistol and Fluellen provide a little humour to lighten this rather brooding and reflective scene. We can anticipate sparks when these two meet again.

There is simple comedy in Fluellen's long-winded explanation as to why Gower should keep quiet. Gower is the straight man in these scenes involving the captains.

We are given some insight into the views of the common soldiers and we are reminded that their deaths would leave their families poor.

Our respect for Henry grows because we know he takes his responsibilities seriously and is not merely pursuing his own gain and honour.

He speaks to his soldiers man to man and does not take refuge in his rank and power, even when he is threatened with violence.

Henry is pious. He prays sincerely and has tried to make amends for his father's sins.

This scene provides a slow and sombre prelude to the excitement and activity of the battle.

Scene 2

The French go into battle

In the French camp the next morning, the French lords are preparing confidently for battle. A messenger informs them that the English army is in position. The Constable remarks that there are scarcely enough English to give them a decent battle. He fears that the enemy will be so overwhelmed by their approach that they will surrender without a fight. The Earl of Grandpré enters and calls upon the French nobles to hurry. He describes the English as miserable and disgusting in their appearance. The Dauphin mockingly suggests that they feed and clothe the enemy before they fight them. Led by the Constable they head for the battlefield.

Comment

Henry is a competent general and has drawn up his forces before the French are ready. He has chosen the ground where they will fight.

We are again reminded of the great French advantage in numbers and the weakness of the English forces.

Once again, the arrogance and contempt of the French lords means that the audience look forward to their defeat and humiliation.

Scene 3

Henry inspires the English leaders

The English leaders are assembled before the battle. We hear that King Henry has gone to view the enemy forces. His army is outnumbered by five to one. The Earl of Salisbury leaves to take up his position and bids a friendly farewell to the others.

When the King returns, Westmorland says he wishes they had another ten thousand men. Henry disagrees and points out that the smaller their army the greater the honour will be if they win. To emphasise this point he offers free passage home for any man who wishes to leave. He tells them that this is the feast day of St Crispian and promises that those who survive will never forget it. On the anniversary they will be proud to show their wounds and tell the story of the battle. It will be passed down in history and they will be envied by those who were not present.

Salisbury arrives to announce that the French are ready to attack. He is followed by the herald, Montjoy, with another enquiry about Henry's ransom price should he be captured. Henry offers nothing but his bones, if the French can manage to kill him. He sends a defiant reply to the Constable of France saying that his soldiers may look poor and dirty but their hearts are ready and willing. He tells Montjoy not to come asking about ransom again.

Before they all leave for the battlefield, Henry grants the Duke of York's request to command the main body of troops.

Comment

Relationships between Henry and his nobles are friendly and caring.

Henry cleverly makes a virtue of their small numbers to inspire confidence in his followers.

He encourages them to think of themselves as privileged to be present. They are about to make history. He also flatters them by calling them his brothers.

He generously allows the Duke of York the honour of leading the main body of his troops.

y

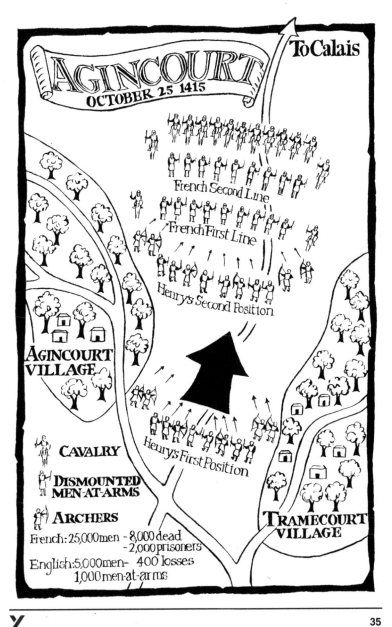

To Calais

AGINCOURT
OCTOBER 25 1415

French Second Line

French First Line

Henry's Second Position

AGINCOURT
VILLAGE

Henry's First Position

CAVALRY

DISMOUNTED
MEN-AT-ARMS

ARCHERS

TRAMECOURT
VILLAGE

French: 25,000 men - 8,000 dead
- 2,000 prisoners
English: 5,000 men - 400 losses
1,000 men-at-arms

Scene 4

Pistol captures a French soldier

In a quiet part of the battlefield, Pistol captures a French soldier. They are unable to understand each other. Pistol misinterprets the Frenchman's words, and threatens him while demanding a ransom. The Boy acts as interpreter and the prisoner promises to pay two hundred crowns. Pistol leaves with his captive and the Boy comments on Pistol's loud-mouthed cowardice. We hear that Nym has been hanged as well as Bardolph. The Boy returns to the army's baggage train which, he says, is vulnerable to French attack.

Scene 5

During the battle, the Dauphin and the other French leaders witness with horror and shame the defeat of their forces. In despair they throw themselves into the fight hoping to salvage their honour by dying in battle.

Comment

The French leaders bitterly remember their boasts and how confident they were of victory. The Dauphin's suggestion that they should stab themselves is almost laughable.

They do not enter the battle to try to organise their forces but merely for reasons of damaged pride. This is a pointless act.

Scene 6

The death of two English nobles

King Henry enters with his soldiers and some prisoners. He says the battle is going well but there are still French troops opposing them. Exeter arrives with a moving description of how the Duke of York was killed along with his close friend the Earl of Suffolk. A trumpet signals that the French have regrouped and the King gives orders for his men to kill their prisoners.

Comment
The account of the deaths of the two nobles emphasises the friendship and brotherhood among the English.

There is dramatic tension when the trumpet sounds, just when we thought the battle was won.

Henry has very practical reasons for ordering the death of the prisoners. He has a small army and he does not want his soldiers to be hindered by their captives or distracted by thoughts of ransom.

Scene 7
On another part of the battlefield, Fluellen and Gower are outraged that some of the French have attacked the English baggage train and killed the boys. They praise Henry's action in having the French prisoners killed. Fluellen is proud of Henry's Welsh connections and compares him with Alexander the Great.

Henry enters, having beaten off the latest attack. The English have taken more prisoners, including the Duke of Bourbon. He sees more French soldiers and sends a message to say that if they neither come and fight nor retreat then he will kill these prisoners and attack without mercy.

The English have won the battle
Montjoy arrives to ask permission for the French to retrieve their dead. He says the victory belongs to Henry, who immediately praises God.

Fluellen reminds Henry of the good service of the Welsh soldiers in a previous war and Henry acknowledges Fluellen as a fellow countryman.

The King sees Williams, the soldier he had quarrelled with the previous night. Williams does not recognise Henry and says he is looking for the man who wears his glove as a token so that he can box his ears. Henry, for a joke, sets up Fluellen with the glove but sends

Warwick and Gloucester after him to see that no harm comes of it.

Scene 8

Fluellen, acting on Henry's information, denounces Williams as a traitor, but Henry intervenes before things take a serious turn. He gives Williams a glove full of gold in compensation.

The dead are counted

Henry reads out a list of the French noblemen who have been taken prisoner and those who are dead. He then reads out the English losses which are very small. Again Henry thanks God, to whom he gives all credit. He gives orders for prayers to be sung before the army returns to England.

Test (Act IV)

a Fill in the blanks

The night before the battle of .... , King Henry visits his soldiers in disguise. He borrows a cloak from Sir .... He talks to three soldiers and argues with one, a man named ....

In the morning at the French camp the .... complains there are too few English for a decent fight.

Henry tells his soldiers they are lucky to be there. He says it is the feast day of St .... and people will always remember the day of the battle.

During the battle the .... and the other French leaders are horrified to see how they are being defeated. The Duke of Exeter tells the King that the Duke of .... has been killed along with his friend the Earl of .... The French attack again and Henry orders his men to kill the ....

.... arrives and confirms the battle is over. Henry forbids boasting and gives credit to .... for the victory.

b Give modern words for these words used by Shakespeare

1	umbered (IV.Prologue.9)	6	haggled (IV.6.11)
2	coxcomb (IV.1.79)	7	skirr (IV.7.60)
3	wots (IV.1.279)	8	choler (IV.7.176)
4	coz (IV.3.73)	9	forsworn (IV.8.13)
5	englutted (IV.3.83)	10	of good sort (IV.8.76)

C | Quiz

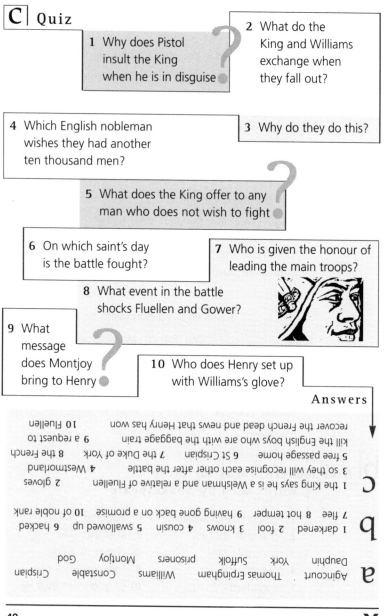

1 Why does Pistol insult the King when he is in disguise

2 What do the King and Williams exchange when they fall out?

4 Which English nobleman wishes they had another ten thousand men?

3 Why do they do this?

5 What does the King offer to any man who does not wish to fight

6 On which saint's day is the battle fought?

7 Who is given the honour of leading the main troops?

8 What event in the battle shocks Fluellen and Gower?

9 What message does Montjoy bring to Henry

10 Who does Henry set up with Williams's glove?

Answers

c
1 the King says he is a Welshman and a relative of Fluellen   2 gloves
3 so they will recognise each other after the battle   4 Westmoreland
5 free passage home   6 St Crispian   7 the Duke of York   8 the French kill the English boys who are with the baggage train   9 a request to recover the French dead and news that Henry has won   10 Fluellen

b
1 darkened   2 fool   3 knows   4 cousin   5 swallowed up   6 hacked   7 flee   8 hot temper   9 having gone back on a promise   10 of noble rank

a
Agincourt   Thomas Erpingham   Williams   Constable   Crispian   Dauphin   York   Suffolk   prisoners   Montjoy   God

Act V

Chorus

We are told that Henry returns to England by way of Calais and receives an enthusiastic welcome. The Holy Roman Emperor visits England to negotiate a peace and eventually Henry returns to France.

Comment

The Chorus passes quickly over a historical period of some years. Shakespeare omits a number of events that he does not wish to include in the play.

Scene 1

Fluellen and Pistol exchange insults

Gower asks Fluellen why he is wearing his leek when St David's day is past. Fluellen replies that he does so to provoke Pistol who has insulted him. Pistol arrives and Fluellen beats him and forces him to eat the leek while Gower denounces him as a coward. When the captains leave, Pistol declares he will return to England to live by pimping and stealing. He will tell people that the scars he received from Fluellen are war-wounds.

Comment

Fluellen's language and Pistol's overblown **parody** (see Literary Terms) of heroic verse provide much of the humour in their encounters.

The serious and responsible Gower approves of this punishment of the cowardly and insolent rogue and supports the Welshman.

Pistol is the last survivor of Henry's old drinking cronies. He disappears into the criminal underworld of London.

Scene 2

At the French court, King Henry, accompanied by his nobles, is welcomed by the French King and his Queen. The Duke of Burgundy describes how warfare has laid waste much of France. Henry says that the French must

King Henry and the French King talk

agree to his demands if they want peace. The French King says he will look at these terms once more and give his answer. Henry sends the Duke of Exeter and other nobles to discuss the treaty. He is left with Princess Katherine and her maid.

Henry talks to Princess Katherine

Henry asks Katherine if she will have him as a husband. He claims to be nothing more than a simple soldier, a man of action and that he is unable to court her with fine words. Katherine speaks partly in French and partly in broken English. She agrees to marry him if her father wishes it. Henry assures her that he does and persuades her to allow him to kiss her.

When the others return, the Duke of Burgundy teases Henry. The French have agreed to the English demands, including Henry's marriage to Katherine, and Henry is declared heir to the French throne. The French King and Queen express the hope that the marriage will bring unity and peace to the two countries.

Comment   Burgundy's speech reminds us of the real destruction and suffering caused by the war.

King Charles of France is again seen to be slow to make up his mind. This contrasts with Henry's decisive and determined nature.

It is hard to believe Henry's claim to be poor with words when we have witnessed his skill when encouraging his army, but perhaps we should admire him for his modesty.

All Henry's demands have been granted. The play ends with his complete success.

Epilogue   The Chorus apologises for the humble efforts of the author and once again for the limitations of the small theatre in the presentation of such glorious events. He reminds the audience that Henry's gains were lost during the reign of his son, Henry VI.

Test (Act V)

a Fill in the blanks

Captain .... meets Fluellen who is wearing a .... because he wants to pick a quarrel with Pistol who has insulted him for being Welsh. Pistol is beaten by .... and forced to eat the .... He decides to go back to .... and live by ....

At the French court, the Duke of .... describes how the war has caused great damage and hardship in .... Henry leaves the Duke of .... to settle the peace treaty with the French and asks to be left alone with .... He asks her to .... him. She says she will if her .... wishes it.

b Give modern words for these words used by Shakespeare

1 scald (V.1.5)
2 bedlam (V.1.19)
3 gleeking and galling (V.1.74)
4 basilisks (V.2.17)
5 greenly (V.2.143)
6 scambling (V.2.202)
7 paction (V.2.359)
8 mangling (Epilogue.4)
9 starts (Epilogue.4)
10 infant bands (Epilogue.9)

C Quiz

1 Why is Gower surprised to see Fluellen wearing a leek

2 Why is Fluellen wearing the leek?

3 How does Gower describe Pistol when he arrives?

4 What does Fluellen tell Pistol he must do?

5 What does he do when Pistol refuses?

6 How does Pistol intend to explain his cuts and bruises?

7 What does Pistol plan to do

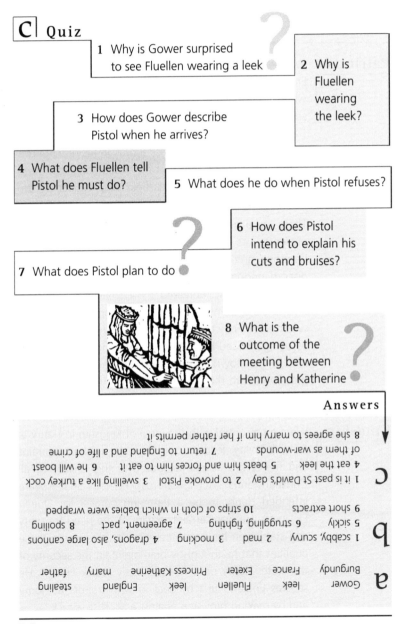

8 What is the outcome of the meeting between Henry and Katherine

Answers

C
1 it is past St David's day 2 to provoke Pistol 3 swelling like a turkey cock 4 eat the leek 5 beats him and forces him to eat it 6 he will boast of them as war-wounds 7 return to England and a life of crime 8 she agrees to marry him if her father permits it

b
1 scabby, scurvy 2 mad 3 mocking 4 dragons, also large cannons 5 sickly 6 struggling, fighting 7 agreement, pact 8 spoiling 9 short extracts 10 strips of cloth in which babies were wrapped

a
Burgundy France Exeter Princess Katherine marry father
Gower leek Fluellen leek England stealing

Commentary

Themes

Patriotism

We are reminded several times in the play of previous English exploits in France. The Battle of Crécy, 1346, when the French were defeated by Edward III and his son, the Black Prince, is mentioned by the Archbishop of Canterbury in Act I, Scene 2, and by King Charles in Act II, Scene 4. The words of the Chorus in his descriptions of the army's preparations for the expedition (Act II), and Henry's speeches before Harfleur and Agincourt are calculated to rouse patriotic feelings in the audience.

There are a number of ways in which the English are presented as being superior to their enemies. The harmony among the English is contrasted with the discord among the French. The French are shown as vain and incompetent, defeated by a small, sickly English army. At one point Henry boasts that one Englishman is worth three Frenchmen. Shakespeare shows the English as being civilised because they spare Harfleur, when in reality, the town was sacked. In the play we are presented with the view that God is on the side of the English.

Kingship

We are presented with the ideal of kingship in Henry V. Piety, humility, learning, courage, leadership, restraint and mercy are all demonstrated in this 'mirror of all Christian kings' (Act II, Chorus). Perhaps Shakespeare intended Henry to be a flattering parallel for Queen Elizabeth. He was certainly aware of the need for unity and stability in his own time and would promote those qualities that he thought would maintain the security of the state. Henry does not recklessly attack France. He secures England first by dealing with traitors at home and by making provision against a Scottish attack.

Warfare

In the Chorus's description of the preparations for invasion, at the beginning of Act II, we are given some idea of the excitement generated by the prospects of the glory and honour to be won in battle. Before Agincourt Henry tells his troops that they will be respected and envied for the rest of their lives if they survive. Even if they die, their names will live for ever.

We also see that war attracts criminals and parasites, like Pistol, Bardolph and Nym, who go only to steal. As Pistol says, 'Let us to France, like horse-leeches, my boys, To suck, to suck, the very blood to suck!' (Act II, Scene 3).

Henry's speech to the Governor of Harfleur (Act III, Scene 3), gives some indication of the horrors involved in the sack of a town.

The night before Agincourt, Williams talks about the hardships suffered by the families of poor soldiers. After Agincourt, the Duke of Exeter gives an account of the bloody deaths of Suffolk and York (Act IV, Scene 6). Burgundy, in Act V, Scene 2, describes the devastation caused by the war in France and regrets that the peaceful pursuits of the arts and learning have been abandoned.

Despite the darker side of war, *Henry V* is a patriotic celebration of the English triumph.

Love and Friendship

One of the merits of the English side is the friendship between the leaders. Henry has affectionate words for Sir Thomas Erpingham and refers to him as 'old heart' (Act IV, Scene 1). Bedford and Exeter bid Salisbury a fond farewell before Agincourt, and we hear how, in the battle, the Duke of York kissed his dead friend Suffolk and died alongside him.

Henry extends his friendship to include all his soldiers and there is a general feeling of good fellowship in the English army.

The love between Henry and Katherine is not altogether convincing. Henry does tell Katherine he loves her, but he is clearly not about to die of it. Katherine agrees to marry him, but she does not have much choice. Theirs is, first and foremost, a political union.

Characters

King Henry

Strong

Brave

Devout

Persuasive

Plain-spoken

Charismatic

Henry dominates the play and completely overshadows the other characters. His words make up about a third of the text.

Taken at face value it seems that Shakespeare has presented us with his view of the ideal monarch, 'the mirror of all Christian kings' (Act II, Chorus).

Henry is a devoutly religious man. He seeks the approval and support of the Church before waging war. He prays sincerely, entrusting his enterprise to God's will and refusing to take credit for the victory at Agincourt. After the battle he orders the singing of prayers and psalms in thanks to God.

Henry's physical courage is never in doubt. We see him leading his men at the siege of Harfleur and hear that he has been in personal combat at Agincourt.

As a leader of men Henry has wonderful insight. He encourages his nobles with references to their forefathers' deeds and flatters his men that he sees noble qualities in them. He reinforces their loyalty with talk of brotherhood and friendship and he leads by example. He refuses to arrange a ransom for himself. The Chorus tells us that the night before Agincourt he went around the English camp, inspiring his soldiers with confidence by his friendly words and cheerful manner.

He is a skilful military commander and avoids useless loss of life. At Harfleur his eloquent warning persuades the Governor to surrender the town.

In matters of state Henry is firm and decisive. His reply to the Dauphin's tennis balls insult is angry but dignified. He listens to the advice of others and considers such practical issues as the danger of a Scottish attack.

He dispenses justice in a fair and impartial manner. The three traitors are condemned because they have threatened the safety of the kingdom. He can be generous, as when he orders the release of the drunk who has shouted insults about him.

Henry has qualities that encourage us to believe in him as a human being. His sense of humour is demonstrated in the trick he plays on Fluellen and Williams. He is awkward and blunt when speaking to Katherine and is unable to court her with conventional flowery phrases and compliments.

It is possible to take a more negative view of Henry and some critics have described him as a cynical, ruthless manipulator. His piety can be viewed as a front which masks his ambition.

We may think him cold-hearted as he has turned his back on his old drinking companions. We hear complaints that he has broken Falstaff's heart and he shows no emotion at the report of Bardolph's execution.

However, there is no real evidence to support the view that King Henry is wilfully deceiving people about his motives and his piety. The Chorus, who we may think of as expressing the views of the author, is always positive about Henry and full of praise for 'This star of England' (Epilogue).

Pistol

One of the old low-life companions of Henry's youth, Pistol goes to France to profit from the war by thieving. He is a braggart and a coward who receives his just deserts at the hands of Fluellen. He provides much of the humour in the play through his speech, his cowardly behaviour and his encounters with Fluellen.

Bardolph

Bardolph, another of the low-life companions, is notable for his red nose, apparently the result of drinking. He is hanged for stealing from a church, which causes a dispute between Pistol and Fluellen.

Nym

Nym is the third member of this gang. He does not say much but has a few catch-phrases such as, 'that's the humour of it'. He, too, is hanged for stealing.

The Boy

The Boy is an unwilling party to the thieves' schemes. He goes to France as their servant after his master, Falstaff, dies. He does not wish to follow the thieves in a life of crime. The fact that they have attempted to corrupt this youth affects the audience's attitude to them. Sadly, we must assume that the Boy is killed when the French attack the baggage train in Act IV.

Fluellen

Professional

Talkative

Loyal

The Welsh captain is a serious-minded professional soldier. His version of the English language provides some simple humour. He is comical when he tries to hold discussions on the theory of warfare in the midst of battle. His peculiar English, combined with his use of learned expressions, results in some very amusing passages.

He is a brave soldier and despises cowards like Pistol. He is particularly proud of his nationality and takes great delight in King Henry's acknowledgement of his own Welsh connections.

Gower

The English captain is an honest even-tempered soldier. He seems to have the respect of the other captains and acts as a straight man to Fluellen in a number of comic situations.

Macmorris and Jamy

These two captains appear only in Act III, Scene 2. Macmorris, the Irish captain, is quick-tempered and proud. He is a great believer in mines and gunpowder and he quarrels with Fluellen.

Jamy, the Scottish captain, is thoughtful and seems willing to discuss theory with Fluellen. Both captains speak in a comic version of their regional dialects.

The English soldiers

Bates, Court and Williams are three common soldiers whom Henry visits in disguise the night before Agincourt. They are thoughtful, plain-spoken men. Williams is the most outspoken of the three and eventually quarrels with Henry. After the battle, when Henry reveals his identity, he still speaks up for himself and excuses himself in a dignified way. We do not see any French noble speaking to a common soldier and we hear references to mercenary troops in their army.

The Traitors

Cambridge, Scroop and Grey all express remorse and accept their punishment when they are exposed. It seems that they are so dazzled by Henry's perfection that they are glad to be caught.

The Churchmen

The Archbishop of Canterbury and the Bishop of Ely are two schemers who are concerned with protecting the property and assets of the Church. It seems that they are happy to encourage Henry to invade France and will even finance the venture as it will keep him from introducing the proposed heavy taxation of Church property.

Exeter

The Duke of Exeter, Henry's uncle, is a staunch and loyal supporter of the young King. Henry regards him as being utterly reliable and leaves him in charge of Harfleur (Act III, Scene 3), after it has been captured. We hear of his bravery at the bridge from Fluellen in Act III, Scene 6. He is one of the nobles Henry sends to settle the treaty in Act V, Scene 2 while he talks to Katherine.

King Charles of France

Weak
Indecisive
Cautious
Fearful

The French King is cautious and indecisive. He asks for time to consider Henry's demands in Act II, Scene 4, and again in Act V, Scene 2. He does not seem at all confident in the face of the English threat and refers to previous French defeats at the hands of

Edward III. He eventually gives in to all of Henry's demands.

Princess Katherine

Katherine is a lively, intelligent girl. She would have been fourteen at the time of Agincourt and eighteen when she became engaged to Henry. We see her sense of fun when she is attempting to learn English in Act III, Scene 4. She provides light relief in this scene between the serious events of the war. She is an obedient daughter as she agrees to marry Henry only if her father wishes it.

The Dauphin

The Dauphin is vain and overconfident. He dismisses Henry as a mere playboy and sends him the insult of the tennis balls. He boasts about his horse and about what he will do in the battle. However, he is almost comical when he suggests stabbing himself when the French are losing the fight. He does not have the confidence of the other French leaders, particularly the Constable of France.

The Constable of France

The Constable of France is a voice of reason among the French. He cautions them against dismissing Henry as an idle youth. He expresses a poor opinion of the Dauphin's courage before the battle and admits to a grudging sympathy for Henry.

Montjoy, the Herald

Henry respects Montjoy for his courage and for the dignified and loyal way he carries out his duties.

Language & style

Shakespeare basically uses three styles of writing in his plays: **poetic verse** **blank verse** and **prose** (see Literary Terms).

Poetic verse

Poetic verse uses pairs of rhyming lines (**rhyming couplets** – see Literary Terms) and has a strong rhythm.

The most outstanding examples of poetic verse in *Henry V* are spoken by the Chorus.

Now all the youth of England are on fire,
And silken dalliance in the wardrobe lies.
Now thrive the armourers, and honour's thought
Reigns solely in the breast of every man.
They sell the pasture now to buy the horse,
Following the mirror of all Christian kings
With winged heels as English Mercuries.

Here the Chorus is suggesting the excitement and pride with which the English are preparing for war. The passage is full of inspiring and noble images with references to 'fire', 'honour', and the 'winged heels' of Mercury, messenger of the Greek gods.

Shakespeare also uses a **parody** of poetic verse in the speeches of the cowardly and boastful Pistol.

O braggart vile and damned furious wight,
The grave doth gape, and doting death is near;
(II.1.61)

Blank Verse

Blank verse does not rhyme, except sometimes in the last two lines of a speech to emphasise something. It has the same rhythm or **metre** of five **iambs** (see

Literary Terms) and is close to the stresses of spoken English.

Let me speak proudly. Tell the Constable
We are but warriors for the working-day;
Our gayness and our gilt are all besmirched
With rainy marching in the painful field.
(IV.3.108–111)

Prose

Prose is language that does not have a particular rhythm or **metre** (see Literary Terms). It is most often spoken by minor, low class or comic characters. Pistol speaks in a **parody** of poetic verse, but his companions speak in prose. When Henry and the common soldiers are talking on the night before Agincourt in Act IV, Scene 1, they all speak in prose.

Henry speaks in prose when he is courting Princess Katherine in Act V, Scene 2, to emphasise his claim that he is only a soldier and does not have any fancy words to win her heart. However, he changes back to **blank verse** when he speaks to the French King and the nobles.

Key Stage 3 & Shakespeare

Examinations

Every Year 9 pupil in Britain has to sit Key Stage 3 examinations in English, Mathematics and Science.

There are two English papers:

Paper I: Reading and Writing Test (1 hour 30 minutes plus 15 minutes' reading time)

Paper II: Shakespeare Test (1 hour 15 minutes)

We are not concerned here with Paper I so we shall concentrate upon the Shakespeare requirements.

Three plays are offered each year for study. Each play has two Key Scenes which are the subject of the examination paper. Your teacher will choose which play to study and more than likely the one Key Scene you will have to answer a question on. For the purposes of the examination you will be issued with a booklet containing all six scenes (two from each play), which you can take with you into the examination. There will be a task on each of the scenes and you will have to complete one of these tasks in the time available.

Read the tasks carefully: they give you a clear structure to use in your written response.

A typical question has three parts:

* A brief description of the scene you have studied
* Details of the task you have to complete
* Some prompts to help you arrange your thoughts

IV.1: What different aspects of Henry as a man do we see in this scene? Think about
  • His relationship with his nobles and his men
  • His feelings about his responsibilities
  • His piety

Careful reading

First read the paper calmly and carefully. Take your time over this otherwise you may miss something very obvious – and discover too late that you have been answering the wrong question. It is a good idea to write the task down as the title of your essay on the top of your answer paper, so that it is always there as you are writing and reminds you to keep on the subject.

Using the prompts

Next write notes beside each of the prompts you have been given to help in your response. You could answer the task without bothering about the prompts – but the mark scheme below will make quite plain how important they really are! The prompts are there to help you.

In Key Stage 3, the examiners really are your friends! They know this is the first time you will have sat a public examination on Shakespeare and that you will be nervous, so they are not trying to catch you out!

The mark scheme

You may be surprised to learn that the mark scheme for each question is identical. No matter which play you write about, your performance has to be measured against everyone else's and this would be impossible if there were six different mark schemes.

What the examiner is looking for is the way you have answered the question you attempted.

A typical mark scheme

Achievement in Key Stage 3 is measured in terms of Levels, ranging from 1 up to 7, with 5 considered as the national average.

It is worth looking at the five statements that a mark scheme uses to describe Level 5 achievement:

* Answer selects *some appropriate moments* from the extract, and the significance of *some of these* is clearly explained

* *Some use of quotation*, though the answer may tend to present a general argument rather than a detailed account

* Points made will *generally be quite straightforward* ones

* Some attempt to link together points to form a coherent argument

* All of the prompts are referred to, but *one or more may not be covered in sufficient depth*

The italicised portions of the mark schemes are the important parts which the examiner will apply to your answer. If you put all these together, you might end up with this description of your essay:

The candidate knows the scene quite well and has used a few quotations which provide a general answer to the task though some parts are not covered very carefully.

The object of this Note on *Henry V* is:

* To help you understand the play
* To enable you to answer the questions successfully

Success at Key Stage 3

The key to success is to enjoy the play. This enjoyment comes from hard work. You must first understand precisely what happens in the scene you are studying. Shakespeare's language can be a little complicated but it is English and it all makes sense.

The first step is to read the scene quite quickly and get a rough idea of what happens. Then go through it more slowly getting a general idea of what each speech is about. If you have difficulties with phrases here and there, don't worry, the important thing is to get the gist of what each speech is about.

A good idea as you are studying is to listen to the words being spoken by a professional actor. Follow the scene in your book as the video or audiotape is being played. Or ask your teacher to read the speech out loud for you. When you hear Shakespeare read aloud by someone who understands it, you will discover that your only problems are individual and unfamiliar words.

Now that you have read and understood what is happening in the chosen scene, you must consider what important aspects of the play are revealed in it.

Examiners do not randomly select scenes for special study: they look for those which are important in particular ways. For Key Stage 3, there are four important aspects which apply to a Shakespearean play:

* The way ideas are presented
* The motivation and behaviour of characters
* The way the plot is developed
* The impact the lines make on the audience

The way ideas are presented

There are many different ways of presenting ideas. If we look at *Henry V*, one of the important themes is kingship. Henry has to prove himself as a true and capable king. Many people remember him as an idle and reckless young man. He shows his worth in several ways right from the beginning of the play and is eventually recognised to be 'the mirror of all Christian kings' (Act II, Chorus). Think about how he achieves this recognition from his nobles, his men, and even his enemies!

The motivation and behaviour of characters

It is often said that we are very good at understanding what makes other people tick, but find it harder to understand what motivates us. But the business of what makes people tick is what we are concerned with in understanding characters' motivation and behaviour.

For instance, Pistol is a thief. He goes to France to see what he can steal. His companions are hanged and when the war is over he sees no more opportunities in France and decides to go back to England to continue his criminal career.

The way the plot is developed

Shakespeare is a very accomplished storyteller. We take that for granted. But think for a moment about the art of telling a story. If it was entirely predictable, a story would surely be quite boring. After all, part of the fun of a story is not quite knowing where it is going next or how things will finally turn out.

The impact the lines make on the audience

Here you are asked to consider your reaction to what is said on stage. Shakespeare was a great writer: nothing is done accidentally. He uses language in two ways: to reflect the speaker's personality, and to create an impression in the audience's mind.

If you listen to the famous opening line of Act III, Scene 1, 'Once more unto the breach, dear friends, once more', you are struck by the power of the line. It is a rallying cry to the English troops. The rhythm is forceful and the repetition of 'once more' adds urgency to the call. Henry refers to his army as his 'friends' and in this way requires loyalty. The French nobles are always bickering and seem to have no relationship with the ordinary soldiers. Now you can begin to appreciate the impact that Shakespeare's lines might have upon his audience.

Using quotations

One of the ways in which candidates achieve high grades in an English literature examination is by the use they make of quotations. The important thing to realise is that a quotation can back up the point that you wish to make.

Here are five basic points you must remember:

* Put quotation marks (inverted commas) at the beginning and end of the quotation
* Write the quotation exactly as it appears in the original
* Do not use a quotation that repeats what you have just written
* Use the quotation so that it fits into your sentence
* Keep the quotation as short as possible

Quotations should be used to develop the line of thought in your essay.

Your comment should not duplicate what is in your quotations. For example:

Henry (in Act II, Scene 2) denounces the traitor Lord Scroop as cruel ungrateful and savage, 'thou cruel, / Ungrateful, savage and inhuman creature'.

It is far more effective to write:

> Henry denounces Lord Scroop as a 'cruel, /
> Ungrateful, savage and inhuman creature'.

Always lay out lines as they appear in the original:

> Before Agincourt, in Act IV, Scene 3, Henry tells his
> men,
>
> And gentlemen in England now abed
> Shall think themselves accursed they were not here

or:

> And gentlemen in England now abed / Shall think
> themselves accursed they were not here

However, the most sophisticated way of using the writer's words is to include them within your own sentence:

Agincourt is a decisive victory for King Henry and his 'band of brothers'.

Use Shakespeare's words as evidence to support your ideas. Don't just include words from the original to prove you have read it!

Literary terms

alliteration a sequence of repeated sounds in a passage of language

blank verse unrhymed iambic pentameter: a line of five iambs

epic a long narrative poem dealing with a great hero, or a work or story on a similar theme

iamb the commonest metrical foot in English verse, a weak stress followed by a strong stress, ti-tum

iambic pentameter a line of five iambic feet. The most common metrical pattern found in English verse

metre this is the pattern of stressed and unstressed syllables in a line of verse

metaphor a figure of speech in which, for the sake of vividness, one thing is said to be like something else; like a simile but without 'like' or 'as'

parody an imitation which ridicules the original

poetic verse a style of speech in Shakespeare's plays using rhyming couplets and a strong rhythmic pulse to the line

prose any language that is not patterned by the regularity of some kind of metre

rhyming couplet a pair of rhymed lines, of any metre

simile a figure of speech in which one thing is said to be like another, always containing the word 'like' or 'as'

NOTES